An anthology

THE ROOTS OF A GODDESS

CM Writer

The Roots of a Goddess copyright © 2019 by Cassandra Mackenzie Wood. All rights reserved. No part of this book may be used or reproduced in any manner whatsoever without written permission except in the case of brief quotations embodied in critical articles and reviews.

Special thanks to Pixabay for supplying some of the illustrations used in this publication.

For every soul that watered my seed,
until I began to grow.

Contents

Dormancy

Rebirth

Growth

Flowering

Dispersal

Dormancy

Dormancy

All at once, I am vacant,
Because I can't remember who I am,
I can't remember who I was,
Before society defined me,
For who I should be.

The Roots of A Goddess

Oh society, look what you've done.
In your unconscious effort to encourage conformity,
You've riddled us with fears and insecurities.
Apparently there's no cure, except for isolation.

Dormancy

I am just a temporary resident fallen victim to the severity of social construct and household virtue. This framework is oppressive, but it is all I know.

The Roots of A Goddess

Inhale.
   Hold.
      Words choke my throat.

Can't you see,
   "Help me,"
      I smile with my teeth.

Curtains closed,
   I am not at peace.
      And my war is silent.

I am a coward.
   How can three words be too much to stomach?
      "I need help."
      "Help me please."
      "I feel alone."

Of course no one would notice,
   It carves itself into the most beautiful minds,
      Until they are hollowed.

Dormancy

A silent disease,
   A silencing disease,
      "God help me please."

Inhale.
Exhale.

Inhale.
   Pause.
      "I'm fine."

"You sure?"
      "Absolutely."

The Roots of A Goddess

No, my heartbreak is not poetry.
It is madness.
I'm breaking down after weeks of security.
I'm crumbing,
Choking on the presence of you in my mind,
Only in my mind.
I'm waking up from an illusion that I was okay.
This pain is not romantic, it is not beautiful,
But it is not invalid.
It is the realest thing I've felt in a while,
No matter its excruciating nature.
I'll be okay.
With your ghost embracing me,
I'll learn to move on.

Dormancy

"It's okay to cry," she says to me.

It certainly does not feel okay when my back slides
down the wall before bedtime, screaming inside
until I bury my sorrows into my knees.
It makes me weak, despite that you say:

"This vulnerability only makes you stronger."

The Roots of A Goddess

A sting.
Sometimes that's what it feels like.
Oh God, I've messed up again.
Words escape me,
Except for the ones that hurt,
And even despite that I let them escape,
They still gather in my mind until I'm battered and bruised.
I've never felt so many eyes under my skin,
Their gazes crawling over me like insects.
I'll hide behind anything,
A wall.
A stall.
A smile.
So help me please,
Though my plea is silent,
Because I've messed up again.
Oh God I'm going under,
It's like I've forgotten how to swim,
Oh God, I've messed up again.
I search for release,
In a drink,

Dormancy

Or a bite to eat and,
I've messed up again.
Oh God, who have I become?
Snippy.
Sharp.
Seething.
Oh God I've messed up again.
I don't know how to speak,
The right words are gone,
And just like that,
Oh God, I've messed up again.

The Roots of A Goddess

This lack of communication breeds assumption.
And it is not all your ignorant fault,
It is mine as well,
And I am scared of my own skin,
Of my own thoughts.
But whose fault is this?
Yours.
I am afraid to speak,
Despite I know,
Something is wrong,
For there's this stigma around it,
And this world is cruel.
So I go on pretending my life is fine,
And I have not a thing to worry about.

I lose myself a little.

Dormancy

And on that longest night,
When the crescent moon is the only light,
I feel myself collapse, into a shell of myself.
　　Where is the sunshine?

The Roots of A Goddess

When you are thirteen years old,
The world begins to tell you how you should be,
good posture dear, don't be lazy now. Keep your
chin up and your skirt down.

When you are fourteen years old,
The world begins to whisper,
If only you were a bit smaller and lighter upon your
feet, don't indulge dear, keep your head clear with
only the aspirations I've fed you.

When you are fifteen years old,
The world begins to suffocate,
You're too proud to taint your image and fabricated
perfection, the unobtainable illusion you've been
taught to reach.

When you are sixteen years old,
The world seems bleak.

Seventeen. Eighteen. Twenty. Fifty-five.

Dormancy

How long will it take for your voice to carry you to greatness, to let go of the doubt of your broken heart and to only be proud of what you are in this moment?
Don't be apologetic,
For you are a goddess, flourishing, existing now in this very instant, today.

You begin to tell the world how to be kinder,
You begin to open your lungs and breathe once again,
And how to be, simply, happy.

The Roots of A Goddess

There's too many broken people,
Hiding behind the stigma of their faults.

Dormancy

And all at once they metamorphosize:

Backless misgivings birthed in the quiet of night.
Their accumulation was my demise,
And as the chrysalids flourish within my gut,
They thrash and pummel and pulsate.
Writhing beneath my skin,
These butterflies depredate my repose.

The Roots of A Goddess

You truly make me feel awful.
And now you're crying as if to say,
"Look what you've done."
It's not my fault that our priorities don't align,
I just wish you wouldn't be so cryptic in your words,
Just be straightforward please,
So I don't have to interpret your sniffling,
And for once,
When you ask for a reply,
I don't give the wrong one.

Dormancy

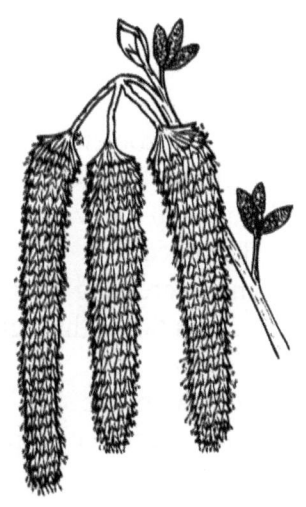

I'm not myself right now,
I'm lucid in knowing this,
But all else is gone,
And I'm floating, I'm merely,
Simply floating within my body,
Something evil has taken command,
And I am trapped within it.

The Roots of A Goddess

I have lost something.
Something I somehow,
Have yet to know.
I felt it once:
A ghost caressing my back,
But it has fallen through the cracks in my
foundation.
I must upturn the soil,
For this ghost tracing my bones,
Felt like home.

Dormancy

To your mother,
To your brother,
To your teacher.
To your preacher,
We display a different facade to each,
And in this method,
We become,
A mass of fractured layers.

The Roots of A Goddess

In a room full of strangers,
She shone bright.
I saw her only that once,
But in my head she's locked, tight.

She is…
She is has become *she was*;
Can it be the same?
Only in memory will *she is* remain.

Come to my place, she had invited,
See the deer through my garden from the den,
I very much wanted to,
But, "next time," I told her, for my time was dear.

We agreed,
I thought after, about her and the grazing fawn on her terrace,
About the yet to be born words we had left to exchange from different walks of life,
And I wondered, did she think of me too?
I longed to join her and watch the yearling over tea.

Dormancy

For too long, I pined,
And she dissolved among them,
Watching a Bambi learn to eat wild plants against
her mother's fur.

Now, when I see a speckled deer,
I will remember new beginnings,
And through a tear,
That stranger full of light.

The Roots of A Goddess

It hurt. After you said it,
Every inch of my body,
Every thought of my mind, felt invalid.
I felt sick with myself,
But even more nauseous,
With the thought of you,
A woman I thought I could trust,
A woman I thought loved me.
How can I learn to forgive and forget,
When you would be disgusted to have me?

Dormancy

Tell me,
If I told you I was hurting,
Would you wrap me in honey,
And put me out for the bees to lick?
Or would you leave me in finality,
Shivering in the dust?
Would you exile me to the forest?
Would you pluck me from the soil,
And watch my petals tumble?
Tell me,
If I told you I needed you,
Would you run and hide?
Would you leave me to burn,
With only my demons inside?
Tell me.

The Roots of A Goddess

The media is seducing,
Feeding us lies until our souls bleed,
Tempting us with deceptions,
And we'll grieve,
Thinking what we have is never enough.
The things you say we should be,
The things you say we shouldn't.
My outcry is too quiet for you to notice.

Dormancy

You broke her. Look what you've done. She's fragmented and scattered, searching for the things she already has. Society has cast shade on her beauty. She refuses to acknowledge that she is powerful, that she is beautiful, she is strong and compassionate and kind. You broke her, you've locked her heart out of reach. You've broken her ribs and she can't breathe. She's disintegrated in the search to be a little of everything. She can't be. But you've taught her contrary, and now, she's broken. Look what you've done.

Of course, you must be right. You're a man after all.

My heels are an invitation to beneath my dress.
The length of my skirt is a provocation for your cruel hands to caress my legs.
The colour I paint on my lips is a silent suggestion for you to touch my breasts.
I'm luring you in with each sip I take.
I'm tempting you to steal my dignity,
I want the attention, I want the attraction.

Of course, this is only what you say, as a feeble attempt to justify your misconduct, your infraction, your intrusion to my womanhood. There will never be a valid excuse for your merciless misdeed.

Dormancy

In the terrible moment when my anger turns to tears, she presses her arms against my shoulders. Through the humidity of my throat, I whimper a salty thank-you of gratitude for her everlasting support.

The Roots of A Goddess

How easy it is to tumble unconsciously,
And for others not to notice.
It has escaped you now,
Your will and better judgement.
At least down here you can find,
Shelter from the social storm above.
It is here you will realize your faults,
And call in salvation.

Dormancy

This world is wicked, hands tickling the hem of her skirt, shoving dishonour down her throat. She's just a girl, and she's been taken.
What has she got left? They've taken the truth, they've taken her words, her body, her sanity.
The world is greedy and run by wicked men.

Help us, please.

The Roots of A Goddess

I'm struggling to teach myself kindness,
Because when I look down at my skin,
I do not see a home,
I do not feel comfort,
I shudder within.
I'm striving to discipline myself,
To only view my body as a temple,
And no matter the changes,
To always worship.

Dormancy

Humans are born with only two instinctive fears: The fear of falling and the fear of loud noises. So why is it that I am riddled with irrational and obsessive fears, dread, horror, abnormal worries?

The Roots of A Goddess

I'm a chronic insomniac,
Internal dialogue gives no ceasefire,
To the vendetta between my thoughts.

Dormancy

She's scared to admit it, her frail state of mind and disillusioned self worth. That mirror is disloyal and yet she has full faith in its truth. She's suffocating in her lack of self worth, and soon, she will drown.

Society is wicked to us. It warps our minds to only see the flaws in our flesh, and to over obsess.

Be kind to yourself.

Dormancy

A heavy tear tickles my cheek. I smear it away, but the action is of no use, as it is quickly replaced by another, and another until my face is covered in a thin sheen of salt. I let my emotions cascade out, in silence, of course.

The Roots of A Goddess

Suffocating, I can't breathe.
In the depths of the ocean, I can't see.
I've been trapped.
You see, the world is the sea,
And society is the monster,
Stealing those last precious ounces,
Of the oxygen I need.

Dormancy

Being hated by *him* is like breathing underwater. His loathing is viscous around me, choking me until the truth spills from between my gritted teeth. I'm burning, in my muscles and lungs. I'm being compressed, wandering without solitude. My bloodstream is inflamed as his judgement collapses around me. I am helpless. There will be no lulling myself to sleep, not with him watching, with him hating. There will be no peace without his approval.

The Roots of A Goddess

I just don't quite understand it.
She is so,
Fragile, yet so,
Wonderful, brave, beautiful.
Why? Why would she want to,
Simply disappear, forever?
Yes, the flowers would have been pretty,
As she had planned,
But there would be no beauty,
In the abyss that would always be,
Her place next to me.

Dormancy

She'll just allude to it,
In cryptic messages,
While she hides behind the pages,
That are her walls.

Here she is bare and bruised,
Writing her wrongs in ink,
But let her words not be misused.
For she refuses to be faulty.

She is not dishonourable,
Corrupt, wicked,
Or blameworthy,
As society would have her think.

For her compassion,
Is commendable,
She is worthy of love,
She is worthy of it all.

Sometimes I feel as if I am only an acquaintance of myself.
I'll watch her, drifting through life in these cyclical phases,
Never moving forwards, only living in the illusion of progress.
Sometimes even, on the darkest of days, I feel the acquaintance becomes a stranger,
I'm lost and wandering in a viscous haze,
It's harrowing, I see my vision narrowing, and so I focus,
On that tapering lighting ahead, golden, golden and glowing,
The warmth pierces my skull for a fleeting moment,
And then, even that, is gone.

Dormancy

I realize all at once, that it's a tragedy:
The giving to those unreciprocating.
She wonders why she is not enough.

The Roots of A Goddess

I'm bleeding emotion,
Overly critical I am,
Wounded in shadow,
I'm broken and bruised,
And oozing,
Lifeblood from my fragile hands.
If there's a God,
Help me please, to simply,
Find, a droplet,
Of peace.

Dormancy

My mind is in chaos,
Because this world has me,
Begging on my knees,
For forgiveness,
For what I am,
And what I am not.
There will be no calm,
In this madness.

The truth is that society profits on our self doubts.
Considering things,
I've probably made it a fortune.
I've bought into the trending lies that convince me,
I am anything but worthy,
And that I should be ashamed for who I am.
Help me.

Dormancy

There's a morbidly primitive madness in my veins:
I'm attracted to the chaos that causes me pain.

Rebirth

Rebirth

Crumbling is not your destruction,
It is your rebirth.

The Roots of A Goddess

In the desolate pit of my stomach,
Flowers begin to take root and grow,
Reaching for the sunshine,
That has become my soul.

Rebirth

I'm tired of you making me feel wrong.
I am my skin and bones,
But I am so much more than what your eyes can see.
I'm tired of you assuming all these words and labels
without thinking for a moment to even consider,
That you might be wrong.
You are wrong.
Don't ever try to convince me that I am a problem,
Because in all honesty,
The world needs a little more love.

My heart stumbles upon itself and I realize, I should not persecute myself for such feelings.

Rebirth

At the tip of winter her roots began to hold,
She grew and dug so she would not be cast astray,
And when the soil gave way, she reached, fingers outstretched towards the sun, that glowing beam of opportunity,
She strove, stretching, hoping, ascending,
Until the leaflets gave way to blooms.
I say she's the most beautiful floweret in that barren meadow,
Of course he wouldn't:
That archaic man still stumbling in winter fever,
He's got a fear of beauty and a lust for cold.

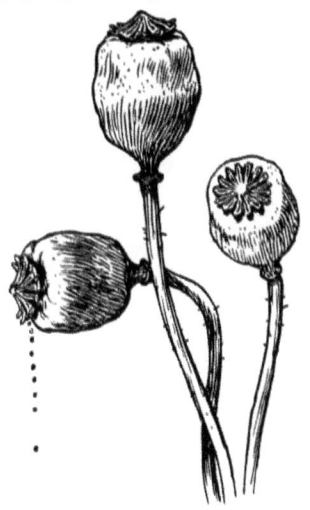

I conceal. I push these feelings to the brink,
These wildly, bold and brilliant feelings,
Until they almost slip, and then,
I'll remember that these varied colours are worth holding,
They are my soul, they are my mind, they are my heart.
And although still concealed, these feelings remain within.

Rebirth

I'll wake before the sun,
In the early rise of morning.
With weepy eyes I'll watch,
Vacantly facing the navy abyss,
In a moment of empty calm.

I've let myself slip, in many ways,
Because I'm ashamed, I'm weak,
I'm my hardest critic and so,
When I'm not pleased, I let go for a brief moment,
And the destruction gets done.
I'm not entirely what I want to be, yet,
Perhaps I never will,
But life is a journey about becoming,
We're always becoming something new,
Always changing.

Rebirth

I've only got two hands
And a world to carry.

The Roots of A Goddess

It is all in moderation.
Water your garden.
Give it sun.
But too much and it will
dry or drown.
So give me space to grow.

Rebirth

Why did I have to justify it to myself?
Just barely twelve and keeping a secret,
Because I was scared.
I shouldn't have to have been scared.

This world is deranged.

How many times will I have to say,
"Don't think about it," and I go numb?
Pushing all these feelings aside,
Like branches of a low forest,
Only these branches are thorned,
They strike sharply when I'm not looking.
A night about,
A night sleeping,
A night drinking to dissolve the pain.
If only it were that simple.
So here I find myself,
Thoughts attacking each other,
Until I'm purpled and exhausted.
And so I call it in for the time being,
But pain does not yield to command,
In fact it seems not to yield to anything.
It is dominant,
And I am losing a war against it.
As I try to rebuild my strength,
And refuel my tank,
I succumb to a firework explosion of emotion,
Of pain,
Again.

Rebirth

Why must I be everything I'm not
Just to please you?
It may be time to cut you out,
But when I do,
I'll carve a bit of myself too.

The Roots of A Goddess

Forgive yourself if you take a fall,
Carry absolution and good virtue in your heart,
And all will be well.
Carry with you selfless generosity,
And tolerance for what you do not understand.
Do this, and love will follow.

Rebirth

Inject me with moon dust,
Because of all the things I wish I could be,
The sky is the most.

The Roots of A Goddess

How dare you assume?
How dare you put your own truth to my words?
How dare you invade my atmosphere,
My most intimate, personal, fragile existence?
Why can't I exist without any excuses,
And just simply,
Be whoever I choose to be,
Without your judgement?

Rebirth

Unhurriedly she walks,
Breathing in the garden air that floats around her head,
She says farewell to the darkness that flees behind the horizon,
And introduces herself to the springtime flowerets.

I fight to pry my eyes awake. Slumber holds my demise, for there is no sweeter illusion than the way you exist in my dreamscape. I'll lay my ear upon your cage and fall victim to the hypnotic melody. At least this isn't reality once more. You took the tiny shards of my essence and hid them up above. I am no skilled scavenger, except when it comes to giving you love. You've reeled me in once more, I am a mere fish taking bait, and that is why I pry to keep my eyes awake. I will not stumble into your depths again.

Rebirth

Upon tidal spines,
I am lost,
Floating aimlessly,
I wash ashore,
To find new beginnings.

Rebirth

Yesterday she did not sleep,
Nor did she the day before.
Her mind was venturing elsewhere,
To lands beyond reality,
To a paradise she would die to visit,
Partially for the oaks and thistles,
But for much more than that…
To feel his papery cheek press against hers,
And welcome her home.

Rebirth

The butterflies are rising,
From the softest, yet wildest,
Space in my abdomen.
They are ready to soar.

Through the tears upon my pillowcase,
And these reminiscent verses,
I love him quietly.

With time I will move on.

Rebirth

Please be gentle,
I'm learning to be strong.

I'm struggling to ignore the voice that tells me,

"It could've been different."

Rebirth

I am my own saviour.
I've clawed my way, bone and nail,
To the top,
From the depths of my weaknesses,
To the mountaintops of my strengths.

Growth

Growth

Although you are not in the place you want to be,
Neither are you where you once were.

Sometimes I feel I am more words than a person. These feelings elevate and overflow into pen and paper. I watch myself, now translated into an abyss of navy lines, and I'll smile in gratitude, that I have found this outlet.

Growth

It began in my core, a constant affliction. It did not ebb with ease. The ache was permanent and in the bitterness, I suffered. My skull condensed in tribulation. I lost density. My colours dwindled. I was no longer vibrant. Days prolonged, and nights abbreviated. I had stretched myself in too many directions, and I became thin and feeble. Looking back, I realize, these were just growing pains.

The Roots of A Goddess

Her cloak was swept away.
She was unprepared,
Needless to say,
For the bleak reality of things.
For a moment, she froze,
Her troubles still within.
But then, the spring arose,
And she thawed.
And with her, the demons returned to the valley,
Retreated from her soul,
And she could thrive once more.

Growth

Tiny quivers lull upon her nose,
Cerise rimmed, brimming eyes,
Downturned, chin wobbling,
Breath shuddering between ribs,
She can't bear the thought,
Of braving life, without her,
Beside her, eternally.
All limbs pull her into a soft embrace,
It's as if this shoulder,
Was meant for her chin.
This woman is her heroine,
This woman is her home,
Her comfort, her love,
Her mother.

The Roots of A Goddess

Love makes you

    Blind.

Giving little p i e c e s of myself,
I am s c a t t e r e d ,

d i s p e r s e d.

I cannot see your flaws,
I see past them,
through your cloudy eyes.

    Are we still strangers?

Suffocating in questions.

I

  sink

    low.

But your arms still reach…

Growth

… and rescue me to the light.

Love hijacks senses.
I have thrown away my guard,
My common sense.
I am exhilaratingly,
Terrifyingly,
Free.

The Roots of A Goddess

It's not feeble to ask for help,
You're not broken, trust me,
Life is a work in progress,
And you may be at the beginning,
But great things are to come.

Growth

Why was it unreceived,
The loving that I needed?
In truth it was no one's fault.
The pace of the world blinds us.
And so, I said the words and,
Gave myself the loving that I needed.

The Roots of A Goddess

It's taken me time to realize,
It is not selfish,
It is brave,
To make oneself your biggest commitment,
And although,
Guilt may weigh me down,
I come first and foremost.
I'm worth it,
Right?

Growth

You reminded me today,
It's been 52 weeks since us.
Strange to imagine how it could have been.

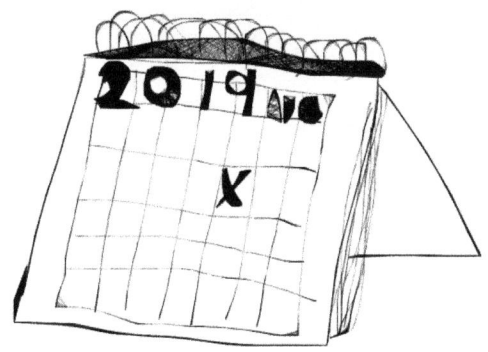

The Roots of A Goddess

He just didn't have the capacity,
So much amiss, it just didn't fit,
I know wholeheartedly,
I deserve the one,
Who has the room, for all of me.

Growth

I give in momentarily, savouring the touch of his slender fingers across my cheek.
My thoughts muddle.
I am frozen, not in time, but in thought.
Once more I am trapped.
Should this connection not feel liberating?

The Roots of A Goddess

And for a brief moment I was back,
To watching colours dance upon the glass.
You half blind gorgeous fool,
Why did you have to conceal it?
Why couldn't you have told me?
Before I was captivated.

Growth

It's hard for me to admit it,
That I was wrong,
That I did wrong,
That I hurt you.

But you must realize you did the same.
In your tiny deceptions,
And little games,
I got hurt.

The Roots of A Goddess

What I am most afraid of,
Is forgetting,
Losing the image of sun caressing your cheeks,
Missing your voice ringing throughout the room.
These things are already blurry,
Feeling your little embrace,
The shake of pride in your shoulders,
With farewell cooling on my cheeks.
These things are precious.
Fleeting memories,
Do not lose the power,
To bring me back to the smell of your jacket,
The stature of your walk.
All of which, are priceless.

Growth

I'm chasing memories,
So that one day,
I won't feel so alone,

The Roots of A Goddess

I don't need your saving,
My thumb dries the salt beneath my eyes.
These tears could fill an ocean,
And so, I put them to use,
Carving tiny rivers into the earth,
Shedding rainfall upon the desert,
Storming my emotions into a wondrous land,
And when my grief is gone and with it my sadness,
I can look at the world I have crafted for myself.

Growth

There is a calmness of mind I find while at sea.
The way the stars are reflected upon the water,
Gives me peace.
I watch as they dance in little patterns, distorting in reflection.

The Roots of A Goddess

Glass figure,
Look at how the light plays with your skin.
What a pretty smile you have,
Engraved upon your chin.

Glass figure,
Where have you been?
Your teeth still smile,
But they're wearing thin.

Glass figure please,
Don't mind the chip in your knee,
You're fragile in places,
It makes you beautiful can't you see?

Glass figure,
Why are there tears about your eyes?
Don't listen to them,
Truthfully, they don't mind.

Glass figure,
I know your joints are stiff,
And your soles are sleepy,
But your limbs stay sturdy.

Growth

Glass figure,
Wishing to fall.
It's pointless however,
You're already shattered.

The Roots of A Goddess

She has a heart of gold,
Encased in lead,
No one would know.

She has a colourful garden,
Its paths unwalked,
And its plants unwatered.

She has a rain cloud in her head,
She's afraid to thunder,
Because no one will dance in her rain.

She's got a heart of gold,
Withering, dulling,
But no one would know,
Unless one saw the value in withered gold.

Growth

I freeze as I realize, there is no denying our connection, my attraction to him, and his lips felt wonderful against mine for that fleeting second. Impulsively, I shake my head and clasp my hands upon the bed. I lean to kiss him, ignoring the alarm in my mind, the blaring warning of toying with muddled times. I want to pull away before I miss, before I lose myself entirely, but my mind is preoccupied with the abyss, of the world falling away from my eyes as they shut and my hands fall from his face to his neck.

The Roots of A Goddess

I am skin,
I am bone,
I am muscle,
Yet I do not know what I am made of.

I live protected,
In a house,
With locked doors,
In a free country.

I should feel free,
But instead,
Life seems meaningless,
I have no cause.

I will make no difference,
I will save no lives,
I will not have a hero's legacy,
Or a warrior's battle scars.

I should be thankful,
And I am,
Yet adventure calls me,
It runs through my veins.

Growth

I crave any danger,
Pain,
Risk,
Anything to ground me into reality.

Take me away from this mundane world,
For millions live worthlessly,
Though worth a number,
But not worth remembering.

I wish to be remembered,
For generations to come,
I wish to start a movement,
One in which I'll fight.

For I'm growing weary of tireless nights,
Of shaky hands,
And a wild mind bound only to this life.

Set me free,
I wish to see what I am made of.
I wish to see my muscles and bone,
I wish to be freely unprotected,
I wish to design:
What I am made of.

The Roots of A Goddess

What gives you the audacity to objectify me?
What gives you the confidence to degrade me to a mere piece of satisfying flesh?
What gives you the boldness to humiliate me for simply being a woman?
What gives you the will to disrespect all that I am?
Of course, we all know the answer:
Societal flaws running in our foundations,
Promoted by headmen and media,
Seeping upon the facades of avaricious young men.

Growth

I think the biggest flaws of society,
Are the secrets it tells us to keep.
Hide the lines of your body,
Hide your silhouette,
Don't tell them who you're loving,
Don't share the memories you keep.
Conceal your vulnerability,
Build up that facade,
And society will love you,
For it cannot see your flaws.

The Roots of A Goddess

I smiled, but only as a courtesy,
Only because I'm obligated to pay my respects
when you praise my beauty.
Despite every ounce of *human*,
Every gallon of *I'm more than that*,
I smile and let you move on,
Trapped in your archaic thinking.
Before I am beautiful, before I am objectified by
your cruel and demeaning desires,
I am brave, I am bold, I am strong.

Growth

I am not a feral woman,
I cannot be domesticated or tamed.
I am wild in the most sophisticated of ways.

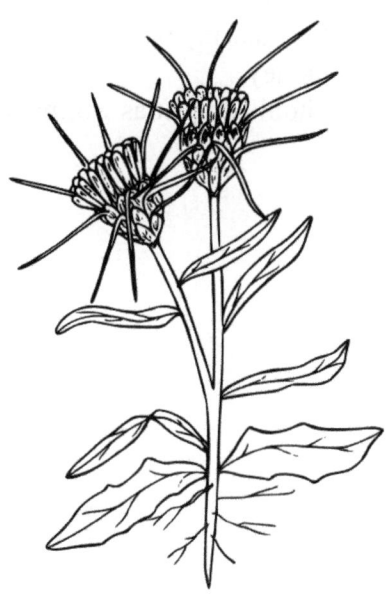

I hope you're not ignorant enough to believe that feminism is synonymous with discrimination against man.
It is in fact, simply a liberation movement for equality.
Because my words, my work, my education, my money,
Should be just as worthy as yours.

Growth

When the flower struggles to grow,
One does not blame its roots.
Instead, the gardener wonders,
How to make the flower a better home.

Learning from this,
I began to pour sunshine upon myself,
Until I began to bloom.

Flowering

Flowering

Find your sunshine,
Take pride in yourself,
Accept initiative for your ambitions,
And with these things,
Grow a wildly untamed flower garden.

With its beauty, inspire the world.

The Roots of A Goddess

The sunshine of his soul rains upon me,
Bringing only fruitfulness and joy.
His warmth encapsulates me in a golden haven,
And never again,
Will I ever be cold.

Flowering

Patiently I'll rest,
Breathing the pollen of morning flowerets abloom,
I'll indulge in a little sunrise, a little golden warmth,
I'll be surrounded by only kind and tranquil life,
And for a moment, perhaps I'll wish mine was a little more simple.

Flowering

You're gonna melt a lot of hearts, he bids me farewell.
I feel so many phases of myself follow him through that door.
Forever will I remember that final salty embrace.

Flowering

There's no time to be wilting.

The Roots of A Goddess

You make me feel like a first snowfall,
Soft and silky diamonds between my teeth.
You make me feel like orange pekoe tea,
A warm sweater atop my skin on the autumn sea.
You make me feel like sunshine in trees,
A powerful energy gifting kindness to the earth.
You make me feel like unwritten poetry,
Happiness at my fingertips and joy upon my tongue.
You make me feel real.

Flowering

Take the time,
To appreciate the warmth of the sun,
Even in winter.

The Roots of A Goddess

And her silhouette is sunshine,
Brushing against my mind in the hours of only moon.
And her soft red cheeks are blooming,
A thousand rose gardens on my hands.
She is a cascading beam of illumination
In a world otherwise dark.

Flowering

While time may escape us,
We can savour each second,
Every moment, fleeting,
Slipping between clenched fingertips.
And although these instances are brief,
They are what gives life substance.

The Roots of A Goddess

Your flesh is soft under my fingerprint,
Like a handwoven cushion,
And your shoulder, is the perfect mould for the form of my ear,
I listen,
to the drumming of your essence,
For a moment,
I am blissfully absorbed into your bloodstream,
And my worries are carried away.

Flowering

The crook of her lip and the drop of a dimple, they water my imperfections.
Life becomes simple.
And in her rain, under her reign,
I feel wonderful.
These faults are no longer pitiful.
I wear them only with pride.

The Roots of A Goddess

Some days are ecstatic,

Saturated with pure joy, I dance to the beat of the songs I love, I jump and twirl on the hardwood of the kitchen.

Some days are euphoric,

Enraptured with poetic verse, I grin to myself and the phrases birth, curled in blankets, with milky tea and my precious kitten.

Some days are perfect.
Savour them.

Flowering

I wish they knew,
Of the rainbows in my soul,
Exploding in vibrancy,
I can barely contain it.
Why do I?

The Roots of A Goddess

There's a hummingbird who lives in a flowery garden and drinks sweet nectar from the supple palm of a maiden.

Thrum. Thrum. Thrum.

His wings beat against the drum of time, powered by the sugary lifeblood of honey.

I am the maiden with supple hands and his garden makes it home within my chest.

Flowering

All of us have reason to love.

The Roots of A Goddess

I brought the sunshine.

He brought the rain.

Together we grew gardens,
From the faults of our pain.

And from the garden we grew hope,
Laying in bedsheets simply envisioning,
The world we were to make.

Flowering

I run my pinky along the white stretch marks on my hips. I grasp my stomach in my hands and I run my hands along patchy skin. These are not flaws. They are what make me human. They make me complete and beautiful and unique. Take pride in yourself. All of you.

The Roots of A Goddess

The sight of her sends melodies through my head,
I'm twirling in a pastureland, with her happiness in
my hand,
We fall among the flowers and our worries go to
seed,
To grow, to reach, to form new things, bigger than
the both of us.

Flowering

There, from across the room,
She's pouring sunshine into the hands of strangers.
And they'll watch, a field of sunflowers following their star.
Her words plant little gardens upon the slope of my mind,
And the flowerets will bloom as I tumble freely for those gentle eyes.
She repaints the world in every hue,
And never again will mine be simply colourless.

The Roots of A Goddess

There is resolution in acceptance,
And that is why new petals continue to grow.

Flowering

And when at last, our lips meet,
My head is an abstract of instinct,
Keeping you close, keeping me warm,
What a sensation it is, to be lost in your arms.

All at once,
Life feels beautiful again.

Flowering

My mind was pacing with thoughts of you.
I let myself walk down a new boulevard,
One of only you, and me,
And life was simple,
Blissful,
How I always thought it should be.

The Roots of A Goddess

I couldn't fall asleep last night,
But instead of insomnia stealing my sleep,
My pulse was racing and my mind was pacing,
With thoughts of you.

Flowering

You found me in my dreams last night.
Never has my sleep been so peaceful.

The Roots of A Goddess

Once upon a time,
I was a seed,
Buried deep in the soil,
With only winter above.

Then,
Came the warmth,
And sunshine filtered through.

I reached for that sunlight,
Yearning for a chance,
To bloom.

From the darkness,
I ascended.

Although the journey was not quick,
I persevered,
Until one day,
I flowered.

Flowering

All at once, I am flourishing,
Because I've discovered who I am.

And she is beautiful,
She is resilient and strong,
And she is ready to share herself,
With the world.

Dispersal

Dispersal

Finally, I have flowered and my blossoms are ready to seed.
I am ready to share the truths I have learned with the growing garden in which I thrive,
And to start new gardens of my own,
As my seeds of wisdom get carried by the wind,
To places I never imagined.

Pause.
Take a moment.
Apologize to your
conscience for treating
yourself so poorly.

There is no progress without forgiveness.

Dispersal

Growth is not linear,
It is sporadic and random,
It is a process of uncertainty and you must be brave to face it.
One does not transform overnight,
Beautiful things take time.

The Roots of A Goddess

Although we often perceive progress as growth,
Sometimes progress does not mean getting bigger,
Sometimes it means taking a step back,
To simply
Breathe in the beauty of the world we live in.

Dispersal

Self harm is not always physical.
Remember this when you degrade yourself into insignificance.
Remember this when you seclude yourself away because you deem yourself unworthy.
Remember this when you scrutinize your figure and your actions.
Remember this always.
Sometimes abuse is hard to recognize because it is a silent figment that we consider a sign of weakness.
Facing it takes courage.

The Roots of A Goddess

These are the words I wish I could hear,
and that I long to have full faith in,
So listen, please:

Have respect for yourself,
Be kind to your flesh,
It carries you through life,
And you get to choose how you carry it.
So appreciate each line, each fold, each limb,
Be gentle to your skin, please,
Have praise for your body.

Dispersal

Let go of what you *think* you care about.
Society will burst you open and shove a million false ambitions into your chest.
You begin to hurt. I'm hurting too.
Give yourself a chance to simply tune in,
Rediscover the full force that is all the traces of yourself,
Because living is the most worthwhile thing you'll ever do.

You may think it's a sign of weakness or defeat for doing less, but if anything, it's a sign of strength.

Dispersal

Remember…

We are delicate,
Like blossoms in the meadow.

But we are also resilient,
Like mighty oaks in the forest.

The Roots of A Goddess

The universe is trying to tell you something,
And I know, trying to decipher its language,
Is in no way easy.
So let me interpret it for you,
The world is worried about you,
And it is just waiting for your greatness,
To shed light upon the darkness,
And make some of the evil,
Become good.

Dispersal

There are some things we say too quietly,
And often these phrases are the ones
That should be the loudest.

The Roots of A Goddess

Be fearless little one,
Face the sun with all you've got,
And absorb all the world has to offer you.

Let the bees help you prosper,
Let the rain wash away your pain,
Let the sunshine fill you with power,
Let the soil nourish your soul.

You see, only with an entire community,
Can a flower flourish.

Dispersal

As the autumn looms ahead,
My petals wrinkle and wither,
But I am still strong.

My seeds take hold of the wind,
So that one day,
They can find a home for life anew.

The Roots of A Goddess

We've all got these arrogant,
Preconceived ideas about,
Everything we're not.
Stop the judgment.

Dispersal

I want you to know that love takes many forms,
But across them all,
Love is kindness,
Love is support,
Love is understanding.
Love is a beautiful thing.

The Roots of A Goddess

There is no such phenomenon as hate.
Just as one can never gain cold,
There can be only an absence of warmth,
And thus one can never create hate,
But only be empty of love.

Dispersal

I'm sorry for your lack of compassion. I'm sorry for your narrow mind. I'm sorry you don't think that a woman can love another woman, or a man another man. I'm sorry you fail to see that love is love, no matter the people. I'm sorry you can't accept something more wholesome and pure than you'll ever have the blessing of knowing. And when I say I'm sorry, I'm not apologizing, I'm simply stating my pity for your lack of understanding.

The Roots of A Goddess

Assumption is bred in the womb of society,
Nurtured and fed by a hunger only conformity can satisfy.
But I am not here to fulfil the appetite of man.
I will not gratify societal expectations,
Only my ambition for rebellion.

Dispersal

Strange, without communication,
We'd never know,
How different eyes, different minds,
See life just a little differently.

Tell me, if a flower lost a petal would you call it ugly? No.

The same goes for people. If someone is wilting, don't you dare leave them out to dry.

People are fragile and they need sunshine and water to recover from the long drought.

Dispersal

No longer will I search for validity of myself,
In the preachings of others.

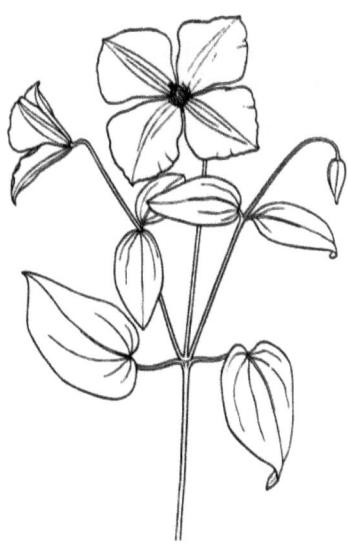

The Roots of A Goddess

I know what it's like.
You'd never know,
But that's because we're both so good at hiding it.
You can confide in me,
I'd never tell,
Because I know how fragile the strongest people can be.
So unburden yourself to me,
And through this liberation,
Find yourself again.

Dispersal

I've realized it in my own faults a dozen times,
That self consciousness fuels anger,
And this rage will tear down the bridges you've made,
Leaving you fragile and feeble,
Wishing you had the courage to admit your own flaws.

The Roots of A Goddess

In order for me to get better,
I think what I needed to hear,

Was that I didn't need to obtain perfection,
To be enough.

Dispersal

We all have scars,
And although they may not bleed,
They are a constant reminder,
Of the things we have lost,
And the things we have become.

Don't you dare be ashamed of where you came from.

Take pride in where you are going.

During the first night,
The flower becomes scared that the sun will never return.

Don't worry little floweret,
The sun will always rise again.

Dispersal

Life is a wonder,
But its end is inevitable.

I don't mean to trouble you,
Only remind you,
That every moment is worth filling,
With happiness.

The Roots of A Goddess

She found peace in her final moments,
As the din of existence began to escape,
She felt herself swallowed,
By meadow flowerets,
And she knew, she'd be home,
One day, to something new.

Dispersal

It goes on.
Life I mean.
So let go.
Let everything go.
Live only now.
Forget the pain.

The Roots of A Goddess

So often we drown ourselves,
Quick, be excellent, make them proud.
But what is there to be proud of,
If you can barely stay afloat?
Don't be afraid, to only dip a toe,
to stay on the boat and only row,
Take your time, for life is only several moments,
And you should cherish them all.

Dispersal

Affection cannot be created or destroyed,
Only reworked and passed from one to another.
So be kind to yourself, and to one another,
Because if the world needs anything more,
It is love.

The Roots of A Goddess

Instead of bullets,
Try blossoms.
It truly is remarkable,
The difference,
Between apology,
And warfare.

Dispersal

Sometimes I sit in our
golden backyard,
And I'll watch the garden
while inventing metaphors,
Like how if I were the
reddening leaves,
You would most certainly be
the autumn I was falling for,
And how life comes in cycles
much like the trees,
And how we should savour
each moment,
Like the birds upon the eaves.
Metaphors make me at peace.

"I love you."
    "I love you more"
"Not possible."
    "It is."

But it isn't you see. In a quantitive formula, yes, for each unit of time we love each other equally and unconditionally. For the past two hundred and seven months we've given each reciprocating love, but you see, those months cumulate to a mere third of your life and I've loved you for the entirety of mine. So you see, when I say I love you more, it is possible.

    // to my mother

Dispersal

You are the sun,
Casting light and warmth upon all before you,
And from your brilliance a thousand glorious gardens will grow.

There's nothing like falling asleep with a smile,
Because I was talking with you.

Dispersal

If there's one thing I've learned,
After taking life for granted,
It's that you should take that risk.

Muster the courage to say "hello,"
Give them the hug they deserve,
Reach for their hand if yours is cold.

If they're everything you want them to be,
They'll be hoping that you do.

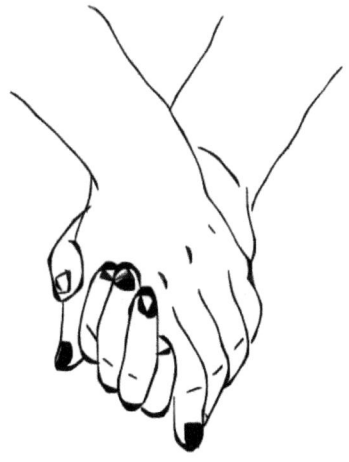

The Roots of A Goddess

I knew he was my home,
Because when I was struggling,

There he was, hand outstretched,
To help me through.

Dispersal

Take the colours of the meadow,
And place them in your soul.

Know what it feels like,
To be home to something wild,
And then, watch yourself bloom.

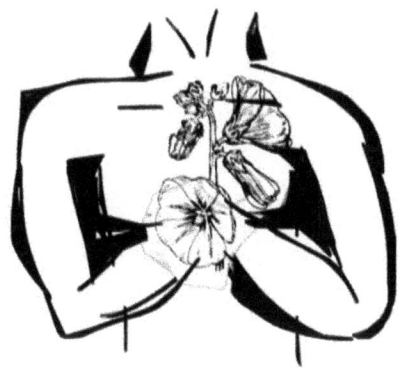

The Roots of A Goddess

Breathe gently, my love.
You deserve a world that's willing to celebrate how
Far you have come.

Don't let others discredit what you are proud of.

Dispersal

Do not settle for a lantern,
When the rise of morning,
Will give you the sun.

The Roots of A Goddess

Be patient,
Because time is the only remedy,
For such pain.

Dispersal

Shed your burdens gently, my dear.
Leave them at your feet,
And feel yourself become weightless.

If you are struggling to water your garden,
Let me share some words of sunshine,

"Believe in yourself"
"I am here for you."
"I love you."
"You should be proud of yourself."

Make the sun rise and bestow its greatness upon you.

Dispersal

Acceptance is the final step in the journey.

You cannot go back and change what has already happened. Time is permanent.

Acceptance is the only pathway to closure,
And that is exactly what you deserve.

Welcome happiness into your soul once again,
Because to it,
You are a beautiful home.

Dispersal

She was born a tiny girl,
With a chorus of rainbows coursing through her,
And she grew wild, unclaimed and undefined,
A vibrant blossom reaching for sun.
As time marched beside her, little thistles grew,
A hybrid mighty breed, delicate and bold.
And now, a violently bold floweret,
She realizes, she is far from her roots.

The Roots of A Goddess

I've spent too long lingering in places I was not welcome,
But through the anguish and despair,
I was taught all I needed to know,
In order to grow.

My only hope,
Is that you take my words,
And use them yourself.

Dispersal

The seed tumbled into conflict.
And from the quarrel, she fumbled.
Fitful tremors unnerved her and,
This lack of consistency molded her into someone broken and wilting.
In this chaos she was rooted,
And when she bloomed,
It was fleeting and fragile.
But as her seeds flew, far from home, her little ones flourished into tiny thriving flowerets.

The Roots of A Goddess

Once upon a time,
I was dormant.
Life was stagnant and I was afraid.

Then the sunshine and the rain arrive,
My roots reach into the richness of the earth,
And I am reborn.

As the soil becomes fertile I begin to grow,
My tiny sprouts reach with determination,
For the sky.

I see the world around me change,
From darkness,
To the vibrancy of this growing garden.

Although there is not sun every day,
There are rains and storms too,
I begin to bloom.

Dispersal

I allow myself to focus on the petals,
The petals that grow from my soul,
Reaching out to embrace the world.
For being so kind to me.

The bees come to visit and take my lifeblood afar,
I realize I am thrumming with gratitude,
For the blossom I have become,
And from such greatness,
I watch new gardens grow,
From the deepest depths,
Of my existence.

The Roots of A Goddess

And now, across the pages of this collection,
You have read my soul.
You know of my inner frictions,
Of my journey to self-love,
Of my quest to worship all that I am.

And I am a goddess,
And my life has just begun.

All that has happened,
Is only my roots.

Please,
If you take one thing from these pages,
Let it be that asking for help,
Is not a sign of weakness,
But one of courage.

If you are hurting,
Do not remain silent.

It only does more harm.

ABOUT THE AUTHOR

CM Writer, also known as Cassandra Mackenzie Wood, is a Canadian poet, novelist and storyteller born in 2002. Cassandra's collection includes her debut poetry anthology *The Roots of a Goddess*, several novels, and short prose. Along with these works, she is committed to sharing daily poetry on her Instagram platform @CM.Writer.

With the power of her words, Cassandra hopes to spread awareness of mental health and social issues that impact the world today.

Ingram Content Group UK Ltd.
Milton Keynes UK
UKHW022248220623
423898UK00014B/1556